Best Friends Make the *Best* Memories

♥

ISBN: 978-1-68088-282-7

and Blue Mountain Press are registered in U.S. Patent and Trademark Office. Certain trademarks are used under license.

Printed in China.
First Printing: 2018

This book is printed on recycled paper.

This book is printed on paper that has been specially produced to be acid free (neutral pH) and contains no groundwood or unbleached pulp. It conforms with the requirements of the American National Standards Institute, Inc., so as to ensure that this book will last and be enjoyed by future generations.

Blue Mountain Arts, Inc.
P.O. Box 4549, Boulder, Colorado 80306

Best Friends Make the *Best* Memories

Written and Illustrated by
Heather Stillufsen

Blue Mountain Press™
Boulder, Colorado

Best friends make
the good times *better* and
the hard times *easier*

A *best friend* is…

- someone to *rely* on
- a *shoulder* to lean on
- someone to *laugh* with
- someone to *cry* with
- the *perfect* shopping partner

Best friends can
do *nothing* together…
and enjoy
every minute of it

They *stick* by
each other through
the *sunshine*
and the *storms*

To *have* a best friend
and to *be* a best friend
makes life *worthwhile*

Best friends make
the best *memories*

A best friend...

- *believes* in you
- listens to you
- is there for you
- *helps* you
- reminds you how wonderful you are
- *supports* you
- needs you
- and most of all *understands* you

Best friends
fill each other's lives
with never-ending *love*

When you are *feeling*
happy or sad,
joyful and excited
or homesick and
heartbroken,
remember...
your best friend is
only a call or text away

Best friends don't have to
agree on *everything*
to be a perfect match

SWEETS
CUPCAKES
ART
PAINT
Portraits
STYLE
CHIC
ICONS OF STYLE

A *true* best friend
will never stop you
from *being*
who you are

Best
Friends

Best friends
encourage you to...

- step *outside* of your comfort zone
- keep your chin *up*
- pick your own pace
- forge your *own* path
- regroup, refocus, and *relax*

Sometimes, walking
with your best friend
is all the *therapy*
you need

musées
à
Paris
meilleurs
amis

Together,
best friends can…

- travel the globe
- solve life's *biggest* dilemmas
- dream
- *hope*
- plan
- be adventurous
- depend on each other
- *talk* about anything
- be honest with each other
- conquer the *world*

Having a best friend
is a reason to be *grateful*
every day

Best friends
are like *stars*…
you don't always *see* them,
but you *know*
they are there

Best friends
are *family* too

A best friend
warms your soul...
and fills your heart
with *happiness*

About the Author

Photo by Christine E. Allen

Heather Stillufsen fell in love with drawing as a child and has been holding a pencil ever since. She is best known for her delicate and whimsical illustration style, which has become instantly recognizable. From friendship to family to fashion, Heather's art demonstrates a contemporary sensibility for people of all ages. Her words are written from the heart and offer those who read them the hope of a brighter day and inspiration to live life to the fullest.

In addition to her line of greeting cards, Heather is the author of five books: *Sisters Make Life More Beautiful*, *Mothers and Daughters Are Connected by the Heart*, *May Your Holidays Be Merry and Bright*, *Life Is Tough… but So Are You*, and *Best Friends Make the Best Memories*. Her refreshing and elegant illustrations can also be found on calendars, journals, cards, art prints, hand-painted needlepoint canvases, and more.

She currently lives in New Jersey with her husband, two daughters, and chocolate Lab.